The History of the Royal Family

Roy Harel

Copyright © 2017 Roy Harel

Publisher: tredition, Hamburg, Germany

ISBN
Paperback: 978-3-7439-3527-3

All rights reserved. No part of this publication may be reproduced, distributed, or transmitted in any form or by any means, including photocopying, recording, or other electronic or mechanical methods, without the prior written permission of the publisher. For permission requests, write to the publisher except in the case of brief quotations embodied in critical reviews and certain other noncommercial uses permitted by copyright law.

Dedicated to Her Majesty, Queen Elizabeth II of the United Kingdom of Great Britain and Northern Ireland and her Dominions

Table of Contents

Introduction	5
House of Normandy	8
House of Plantagenet	18
House of Tutor	31
House of Stuart	41
House of Hanover	50
The Victorian Age	62
House of Windsor	72
Appendices	87

Introduction

The island of Britain has seen its fair share of history, wars and monarchs. The Kingdom of England derives its name from the Angles and Saxons that invaded Britain in 410 after the Roman Empire abandoned the Island.

The Anglo Saxons created a multitude of Kingdoms on the Island and made good use of the various Roman inventions that were introduced to Britain when the Emperor Trajan invaded Britain in 47.

In 793, Vikings from Scandinavia raided Lindisfarne, an island in Northumbria that contained a holy Christian shrine and a treasury, which was thoroughly plundered by the heathen Vikings. This seminal attack started the Viking Age. After the French fortified their land, Viking attention swayed towards Britain. The Danish Vikings would invade England under Ivar the Boneless, and ravage the land.

The Danish forces, or "The Great Heathen Army" were then beaten by Alfred the Great and Ivar travelled to Dublin in Ireland to become King over the City. A truce was signed. England was split, the south went to Alfred and the north became Danelaw, under firm Viking control.

The descendent of Alfred the Great, Athelstan I and Edward the Elder would lead the final push and kicked the Vikings and Danelaw out of England.

England was finally unified and was called the Kingdom of England after the Anglo-Saxons people that dominated the south of Britain. Meanwhile Scotland was unified by the Pictii people (a Scottish tribe that dominated Scotland during Roman times).

England was later invaded once again by Svend Forkbeard, the King of Denmark and Norway.

Svend kicked out the English king and seized the throne. After Svend died, his son, Knut the Great united all his father's realms to create the North Sea Empire.

Knut divided his realm between his sons, and Harold Harefoot became King of England, but his hold on power in England was weak and eventually his son, Harthaknut lost power to the Anglo-Saxon king, Edward the Confessor.

Edward stabilized England and restored peace but his sudden death led to a great power struggle for the throne of England.

That is where this story begins.

House of Normandy

The tale of today's royal family begins way before it was established on the island. Before the ancestors of Elizabeth II came to England, the island was ruled by a succession of Anglo Saxon kings and queens. Their king, Edward the confessor, was a wise and pious ruler, but his lack of an heir made him and his kingdom a target for a war of succession. Edward was, at the time, fearful of the growing power of the house of Godwin, and its head, Harold Godwinson, Earl of Wessex. In order to curb the power of the house of Godwin, Edward was said to have entrusted the succession of the English throne to William the Bastard, the Duke of Normandy, an area of land that was given to the Viking, Rollo, the founder of the House of Normandy, which William belonged to. All things regarding the succession seemed in place, until, King Edward fell into a coma and soon died. Seizing this golden opportunity, Harold Godwinson, convinced the witenagemot, the legislative body of England at that time made up of various wise men, to declare him King over England. Harold's request was permitted, and he was crowned only a day after the passing of Edward the Confessor. At the same time, two major figures rose to make their claim on the English throne. One, was King Harald Sigurdsson of Norway, nicknamed Hadrada, or hard ruler sited a claim to the throne as a descendent of King Knut of Denmark and England. The other claimant was of course, William of Normandy, who claimed Edward had picked him to be his successor.

The three contenders, Hadrada, Harold Godwinson and William

Hadrada was the first to act. He gathered a large army of Vikings and longboats and set off to England in 1066, in the last great Viking invasion. Hadrada landed in Northumbria and sailed up rivers to the town of Fulford. Hadrada quickly defeated the earl of Nnorthumbria in the Battle of Fulford. Hadrada then capture York, but moved in to a camp site around Stamford Bridge. When hearing of this, Harold Godwinson set off with a great Saxon army to defeat Hadrada and unite support of England for his succession. Harold's army met the Vikings in the Battle of Stamford Bridge, in which Hadrada was killed and his army routed, ending the last great Viking invasion.

Meanwhile down south, William landed in Hastings in Sussex with a large army to face off Harold for control of England. Harold quickly replenished his army numbers and headed south to face William. In Hastings, William set up a castle and was given a letter from Pope Alexander II, giving him support. Quickly ecclesiastic branches in England gave support to William as the pope had given him his personal blessing.

The Bayeux Tapestry, a Norman depiction of the Battle of Hastings

Harold arrived in Hastings and readied his army for a violent engagement. The battle began and already William had an advantage as his army was more diverse, including archers and Calvary, and it was better armored with chain mail. The Battle of Hastings became the most important moment in English History up to that time as it ended Anglo Saxon rule over England. Harold was hit in the eye during the battle and soon died, ending Anglo Saxon rule in England forever.

After the battle, William gained control of London, and two months later, the Witenagemot elected William King of England and he forever became known as William the Conqueror. Williams rule is basically the tale of a foreign conqueror that invested all powers of the states into his hand. All noble land owners from before William were removed and replaced by new nobles who were tenants of the King. William spent time removing all Anglo-Saxon nobility in the land and replace them with Normans. In Northumbria and its Viking capital of York, the populous refused to bow to the foreigner William so destroyed all noble fortification and led a mass slaughter of livestock and destruction of crops in the land. William also constructed castles and forts of his own such as the tower of London to keep an eye his rebellious population and the nobility. William also instituted Latin as the language used by officials. William also constructed the first version of a special crown for the coronation of the king which was created in the name and honor of the man who was said to have granted England to the Normans, Edward the Confessor.

William spent the rest of his life reforming England and making his takeover legitimate and strong. William swore in his coronation oath to uphold the old traditions and continue to run England with the courts of Edward the Confessor. William I died in 1087, making his son William Rufus, William II, his other son, Henry was told to be contempt with 5000 pound, would he?

William II was relatively uneventful. He just led the continuation of his father's iron hold on the Country. During William's reign his close relatives Robert of Flanders and Robert of Normandy, a grandson of William the Conqueror set out with Godfrey of Bouillon, Bohemond of Taranto Stephen of

Blois and Baldwin of Boulogne on the First Crusade in 1096, under the orders of Pope Urban II. William II angered the nobility by not producing an heir or marrying at all. William is more famous for his very auspicious death. On a hunting venture with his brother, Henry, William was struck with an arrow during a 'Hunting accident' and soon later died of his wounds in the year 1100. After his brother's untimely death, Henry became King Henry I of England and Normandy. King Henry was a successful Ruler and was very fortunate in his various ventures. Henry ratified a charter, promising integrity to many institutions of England, by promising not to over tax them in any situation. Tragically, Henrys son and heir, William Adaline died when the White Ship sunk. Therefore Henry had to make his daughter, Matilda, the Holy Roman Empress, his heir. Matilda was married to the Holy Roman Emperor, Henry, but when he died, she married Geoffrey of Anjou, a French noble. Geoffrey was known for his odd hats, and he was therefore nicknamed Plantagenet, meaning a hat bearing plants.

Henry I, Matilda and Geoffrey of Anjou

Henry supposedly said to his knights to swear allegiance to his daughter once he died. But when Henry passed away in 1135, the knights and nobility of England were skeptical if they should support a woman and instead turned to a popular noble and Matilda's cousin, Stephen of Blois, son of the great crusader, a French noble and grandson of William the Conqueror.

He was quickly rushed by the army and nobility to Westminster abbey and crowned him Stephen I of England, thus starting a civil war of sorts, as Matilda took up her claim and sailed to England. The war, also known as 'The Anarchy', began and ended in a stalemate that could not be ended, and so, compromise was made. Matilda's son, Henry, whom she had with Geoffrey of Anjou, would inherit the throne after Stephen passed away, even if Stephen did have a legitimate son. When Stephen died, his son was only a boy and Henry was free to take the throne for himself. And with that the Norman Dynasty of England came to an unofficial end as no direct male Norman successor inherited the throne, but the lineage of William the Conqueror survived under new names and titles for centuries.

Henry was son of Matilda, a woman, so he was obliged to take the name sake of his Father, Geoffrey of Anjou.

Henry's rise to the throne established a greater French influence, as Henry had claims on French soil and his House was the House of Anjou, a French noble house which would dominate many of the Kingdom of Europe such as France, England, Ireland, Naples, Poland and Hungary.

The Norman Dynasty of England was an astounding story and drama.

The Norman Conquest would forever shape the history of England and Europe, as the English royal family became entangled with the affairs of the continent.

Their legacy was that of conquerors and foreigners, a quality that would be attached to every English Monarch since.

House of Plantagenet

03   [Sodacan]

The death of King Henry I marked the official end to the Norman Dynasty as any male descendants of Henry I had died. Henry's Daughter, Matilda fought her cousin, Stephen of Blois I, a civil war that had stagnated by this point. A treaty was agreed upon to end the war. It appointed Henry of Anjou, son of Matilda and Geoffrey of Anjou, nicknamed 'Plantagenet', to be the heir of Stephen of Blois. After Stephen's death, Henry became King Henry II and through his complex family history, gained control of England, Ireland, Normandy, Aquitaine, Anjou, Brittany and Gascony, forming an Angevin Empire

04 [Cartedaos]

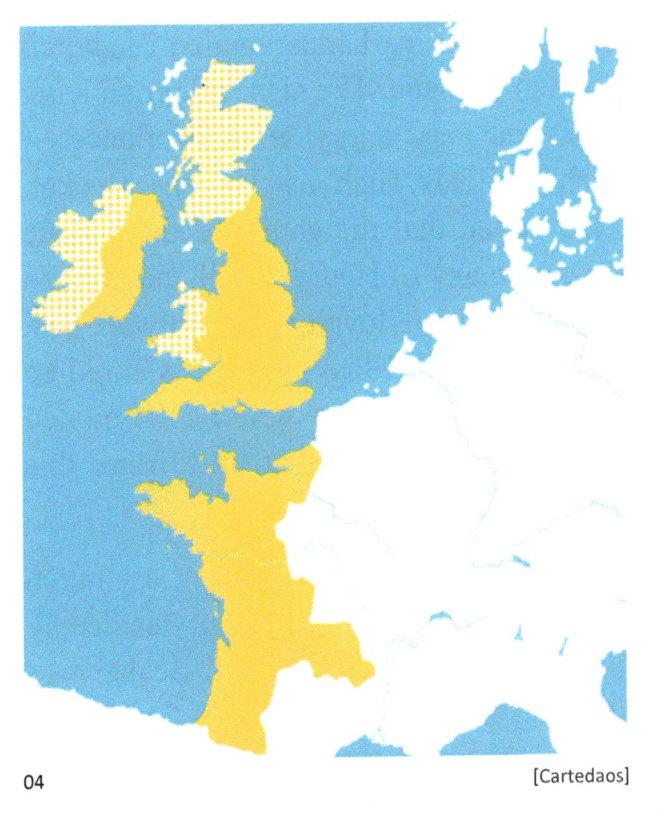

The Angevin Empire, ruled by Henry II and Made up of England, Anjou, Gascony, Brittany and Ireland

Henry learned from recent history that a successor to his kingdom was a vital and important task that should be sorted out. Henry then appointed his eldest son, Henry the young as his co-monarch, a decision he would want to reverse for the rest of his life.

Henry also got his hands tangled in church matters in England. The rash and proud King Henry was very angry at the defiance of church officials such as Thomas Becket. Becket stated that the church and the pope were above any of Henry's civil and laymen laws and that his loyalty was only to god. Henry did not feel that the priests could so easily avoid his grasp and he is quoted saying "who will deliver me from this turbulent priest!" Thomas

Becket was shortly after slain at a Church alter while praying. This action was deeply condemned by the Church and Becket was canonized as a saint.

The Death of Thomas Becket on the altar

The pope quickly threatened to excommunicate Henry and his Kingdom. So, Henry was seen whipped and crawling in front of the pope to save himself and his kingdom from Hell. This action evidently saved England and proved that the Pope was the most powerful force in Europe since The Roman Empire. Meanwhile, Henry's decision to share power with Henry the young backfired. Young Henrys popularity and youth led him to rally his brothers against their father. Only young John was still loyal. The subsequent civil war led to the death of Henry II and Henry the young, and thus middle brother, Richard, ascended the throne.

Richard I was now king but he did not wish to rule England. There was a yearning to Crusade.

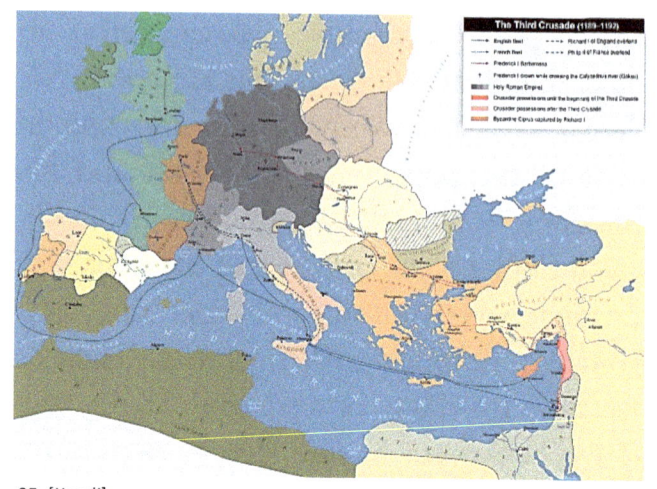

05 [Kandi] A map of the Third Crusade

A Battle Richard I took part in. Richard himself is on the left.

The Third Crusade was a series of skirmishes between the Crusader army of Richard and the Ayyubid Armies of Saladin. Jerusalem was captured for a brief time, but was then recaptured by Saladin. Saladin said that if Richard wanted to keep Jerusalem, he would have to stay there for the rest of his life. The Third Crusade ended in a truce. Saladin would keep Jerusalem but would allow safe passage for pilgrims. The Kingdom of Jerusalem would relocate to Acre, Sidon and Cyprus under a branch of The Anjou Family, King Fulk of Jerusalem would remain on the throne.

King Richard I, the Lion Hearted

Richard traveled alone back to England but was captured by the Duke of Austria and held for ransom. The ransom was paid but,

Richard was fatally shot with an arrow and died. Johnny was now in charge.

'King John is most famous for his agreement to sign the Magna Carta, a document that first defined the role of the king and banned the rule of the king as absolute. King John was incredibly unpopular and was soon the nobility were so disgruntled by John and kicked him out of London. England was invaded by King Louis VIII of France who soon claimed the throne of England for himself. John fled the armies of Louis north and his luck fell more as the chest carries the crown jewels fell into the ocean, never to be seen again.

King John I and Magna Carta [PiaCarott]

Louis' big mistake was not to be crowned in London as quickly as he could. His legitimacy was questioned as he was only acclaimed, and soon that acclamation was also questioned. Louis eventually left England, a loser.

King Louis VIII of France and I of England

The Nobility were now left with John's son, Henry. The nobility instructed a truce to be signed and the son of John, Henry III came to the throne. John's disasters made England vow to never again have a king called John. Henry was more popular than his father. He agreed to respect Magna Carta and was fortunate to rule a stable and prosperous nation.

Yet, Henry supported armies and courts abroad under the orders of his wife Queen Elena. The population rose in revolt. Elena tried to escape down the theism river, but mobs stormed her. She was pelted with rocks by a crowd that shouted "drown the witch!" The country had quickly become ungovernable as peasants filled the land with fear.

Enter Simon de Montfort, the son of a French nobleman and an exile from France. He led his reactionary armies to Westminster, where he called a meeting of representatives from all the Shires of England, in what became, the First Parliament in English History. Yet the country did not support Simon and he was thrown out by Henry's son Edward.

The 'Tyranny of Simon' ended, but the idea of a representative body for the kingdom was established and would never go away.

When Henry Died and his son, Edward, who was out of the country on crusade, came home and became Edward I. He took his name sake from the wise king Edward the Confessor. Edward opened hostilities with Scotland after their king, Alexander III died and his heir died shortly after. Edward took this opportunity to declare himself as Lord Paramount of Scotland and forced his army into Scotland. He was met by a rebellious population led by William Wallace, Braveheart. William was successful but was captured and executed. Edward would fight the rest of his life to gain control of Scotland but the war was ended by Edwards Grandson some years later.

Edward II was a shy and indecisive monarch who was openly homosexual with his squire. This and other actions which led to defeat in Scotland led his wife, Isabella de Valois, the sister of the French king, to overthrow Edward and install his son, Edward III as king with her as his regent. Edward II refused to be crowned without his father's consent, and so Edward II relinquished his throne in tears. Edward II was thrown into a dungeon where he was murdered by being sodomized with a hot iron rod. Edward III signed peace with Scotland and opened hostility with France.

Edward III with the cloak of the Order of the Garter

Edward also expanded the glamour of Royalty, by creating the order of the Garter and building castles for the order.

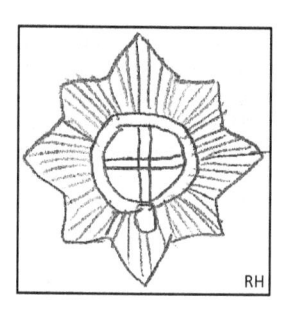

The order of the Garter Star

The Black Death also reached England during Edward III time but he thankfully survived it, but England was ravaged by the plague and it is said that a third of the population perished. Edward also cited his relations to the former French king, being his nephew, as a casus belli, or a reason to invade France and install himself as king of France. This invasion led to the outbreak of the hundred Years war, a conflict which was began to settle to succession to the Kingdom of France. The war was long and draining and was at first very successful due to England's unity versus Frances complicated noble realms who were very unstable and sometimes not very loyal.

Edward III died after the tragic death of his son, Edward the Black Prince. The Black Prince's son, Richard II was now king. Richard was protected by his uncle, John of Gaunt but the subsequent outbreak of the plague, peasant rebellions and his discontent uncles led to his overthrow by Henry Bolingbroke (Henry IV), his cousin, and the son of John of Gaunt.

The overthrow of Richard II led to the end of the direct Plantagenet line of succession. Thus, the cadet branches of the Plantagenet family, the Houses of Lancaster and York would be pitted against each other in a long and devastating Civil War known as the Wars of the Roses.

The war in France would also drag out for the next 75 years and eventually led to English defeat by Charles VII of France.

House of Tutor

[Sodacan] 07   08 [Sodacan]

The ascension of Henry IV began what was known as the Wars of the Roses. Henry IV expanded the war in France and secured the legitimacy of the House of Lancaster.

His son, Henry V, was more prominent and crucial in English history. Henry V led a massive invasion of France as the country was in turmoil due to the madness of Charles VI who had also announced that Henry V and his young son would be his heirs, which did not sit well with Charles' nephew, Charles.

Henry captures Paris, Tours and Reims and claimed his right as King of France, which remained a formal title until the reign of George III.

Henry was incredibly successful in France and his exploits were immortalized in

Shakespeare's historical play. Yet, tragedy hit England like a brick wall. Henry V died in France, and his heir and successor, Henry VI was a young boy. Henry VI was a disaster to England. Under his Reign, the all-important conquests that his father fought years to secure were lost and were made even more famous by the Siege of Orleans by the teenage girl, Joan of Arc, and the tattered French army.

King Henry V and Henry VI

Weak willed, and dominated by his advisors, Henry was convinced to marry Margaret of Anjou, to create a truce between them and France. Eventually, Henry appointed his families rival, Richard, Duke of York as his chief of staff and closest advisor. Margaret apposed this and feared that her position of power was compromised by Richard's rising power in court and in the country. Margaret was more in touch with the Earls of Suffolk and Somerset. Richard was eventually exiled to Ireland for his just criticism of the war in France. But this was not the end! Richard returned to England and ousted Somerset. He raised a large army and caught London unaware. Richard was eventually created Lord Protector of England as Henry suffered an episode of madness, a disease inherited from his French ancestry. While in recovery, Richard was stripped of his title. Richard raised another army and regained his Lord Protector status, which became an inherited title for his sons. Richard was killed after a battle with Margaret's forces and his son Edward, began to claim the English throne. Edward was later crowned Edward IV, and Henry VI was captured after a successful campaign. Yet Edward was briefly overthrown by the powerful Earl of Warwick, who restored Henry VI, however, this did not last. Edward retook the throne and capture Henry VI who died in captivity later. The rest of Edward's reign was uneventful, but when he died his young son Edward, became Edward V. Richard, Duke of Gloucester was regent for young Edward, who was put in the Tower of London for his safety. Edward soon conveniently disappeared, and Richard became Richard III. Meanwhile in France, a distant relative of Henry VI, Henry Tutor set out with an army which landed in Wales, and thus a war for the crown began. Richard set out with his own army and met Henry at the battle of Bosworth, in which Richard was defeated and killed. He is rumored to have said, "A horse! My kingdom for a horse!" while he was being cut down by Henry's forces.

King Richard III

Henry captured London and married Elizabeth of York, finally uniting the Houses of York and Lancaster and ending the Wars of the Roses.

Henry created the house of Tutor and used his time on the throne to legitimize his regal claims. Henry also brought down the power of the nobility by creating the Star Court, a court which was used to intimidate the nobility into staying in line. Henry also sired and heir who would be legitimate in all fields.

Henry VIII became king after the death of his brother, Arthur. He also married his brother's fiancé, Catherine.

Henry VII and Henry VIII

Henry would have only a daughter with her and thus wished to divorce her. His request was denied by Pope Clement VII and Henry took this golden opportunity to adopt Protestantism, acquire all church land in England and make himself head on the new Church of England. Henry also led England to war against the Scottish King James IV and beat him decisively at the Battle of Flodden.

Henry VIII married Anne Boleyn, who produced only a daughter, Elizabeth. Anne was divorced, imprisoned and executed with a sword rather than an axe, courtesy of Henry VIII. The same day Henry married Jane Seymour, who produced at last, a son and heir, Edward. Henry also mended relations with France and its king, Francis I.

Henry created the rule male primogeniture, stating that male heirs are superior to female heirs, this law was overturned in 2014.

When Henry died from an ulstered leg, Edward became King Edward VI at the age of nine. He was said to have stopped the coronation parade line to watch a circus act. Edward also banned his sisters from inheriting his throne and appointed Lady Jane Grey as his heir.

Edward died after a short reign due to an illness at the age of 16. His sister, Mary rushed to the capital and had herself crowned Mary I. Lady Jane Grey was executed later. Mary I was catholic, as she was born before Henry VIII split the Church. She also married the heir to the Spanish throne, Phillip, Duke of Milan.

Mary I of England and her husband, Phillip II of Spain

Phillip and Mary ruled England and persecuted the Protestants of the land, earning the title, Bloody Mary. Mary was also thought to have been pregnant as her abdomen was increasing in size, this abnormality turned out to be a tumor which eventually killed Mary. Her sister Elizabeth no took the Crown. Elizabeth ended all acts that were against Protestants in England and she also refused to marry Phillip. Elizabeth refused to marry anyone as she thought a husband would try to dominate her. She gingerly stated that she was married to England and thus her popularity soured. She also led her country against the formidable Spanish armada invasion of 1589 and commissioned the first attempt of colonization of North America by England in 1587.

Elizabeth I and James I/VI of Scotland

Elizabeth also got her hands dirty as she had her relative, Mary, Queen of Scots executed due to her attempts at claiming the English Throne. Elizabeth ruled during the Shakespearian Age of Literature, which saw the vast expansion of English language and cultural art. Elizabeth eventually died in 1603, most likely due to overuse of a makeup that was laced with lead.

Elizabeth never married and produced no heir and so she adopted James VI Stuart, son of the late Queen Mary of Scots as her heir and successor to the throne.

With the death of Elizabeth I, the Tutor Dynasty came to an end, and England now came under a personal union with Scotland as their King James VI, was crowned James I of England and the Stuart Dynasty began.

House of Stuart

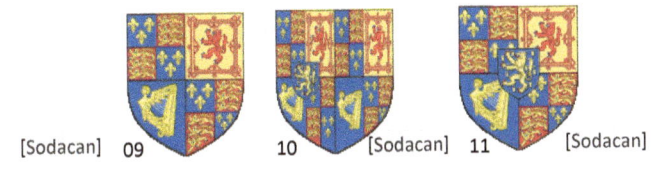

[Sodacan] 09   10 [Sodacan]   11 [Sodacan]

The ascension of James VI of Scotland to the throne of England, by the passing of a Law of succession, ended the dominating Tutor Dynasty as its last monarch, Elizabeth I, had not married and had produced no heir. Parliament saw James as legal to the succession as his great-great grandmother was a daughter of Henry VII Tutor.

Shakespeare wrote Macbeth, a story that was written to show James' legitimacy as King of England

James VI of Scotland and I of England, the first Stuart King of England

James' reign began with much success. The old alliance between Scotland and France ended as Scotland came under the rule of England. The colony of Jamestown was established in Virginia and became the first permanent colony of England in North America.

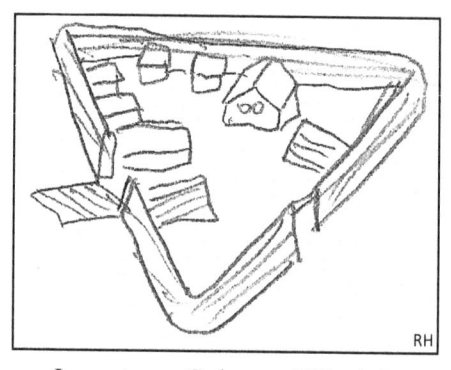

Jamestown Colony of Virginia

Yet James had some opposition. An anarchist, Guy Fawkes, almost pulled off a plan to detonate a bomb that would destroy the Parliament of England and kill James, yet he was captured and executed.

James was also most likely homosexual. James had an array of young male lovers and had no reason to hide his true desires and likings. James also began to push into the

English periphery the idea of the divine right of a Monarch. James stated that his reign was due to God's grace and that he was divinely chosen to rule England.

The English were less enthusiastic about absolutism and the Divine Right Theory as seen from their history of Parliamentary rule and the issuing of Magna Carta.

Yet, James cleverly hid his true power and thus faced less trouble with his subjects.

However, James faced tragedies no man should face. His son and heir died and his shy younger brother Charles now became his heir. During the funeral procession, Charles led the funeral service as James was too depressed and warn down.

James eventually died in 1625 and his awkward son Charles became king. Charles was less clever than his father in hiding his true power and this flaw led to his downfall. Charles bluntly stated his superiority to the other people of his realm and the fact that he was so great he needed no parliament.

Charles begins to dismiss and dissolve Parliament without their consent many times and rules alone. At one point, Charles ruled his realm for more than 11 years without having a Parliament to rule alongside him. Charles also angered England by marrying Henrietta of France, daughter of Henri IV of France, a Catholic. After the Church split, Catholics were loathed and so Charles was loathed.

Charles then demanded that Scotland use the Anglican Book of Common Prayer, which started the Bishops war with Scotland.

Meanwhile, Charles recalled Parliament to raise money for the war, but MP's also passed the triennial Acts, stating the King had no right to dissolve Parliament without their consent.

All of Charles' misdeeds came to a head as Charles wished to arrest influential MP's. This act began the English Civil Wars. Parliament sent a grand Remonstrance to the King which fueled more tension.

The King captured Oxford and the war began as he raised his standard. The Parliamentary army made an alliance with the scots, but Wales still supported the king. The king tried to relieve York but was defeated at the Battle of Marston Moor. This battle also aided Oliver Cromwell rise to importance.

The parliamentary forces created the New Model Army which vastly out gunned the Royalist army. Charles was eventually captured and was put on trial for his supposed crimes against England. It was decided that Charles would be executed and he was beheaded on January, 1649, ending the Monarchy. He made sure to look dignified and strong willed in order to regain support from his subjects even in death.

Charles II, son of the late king, fled to the Dutch Republic, as his relative was the Prince of Orange.

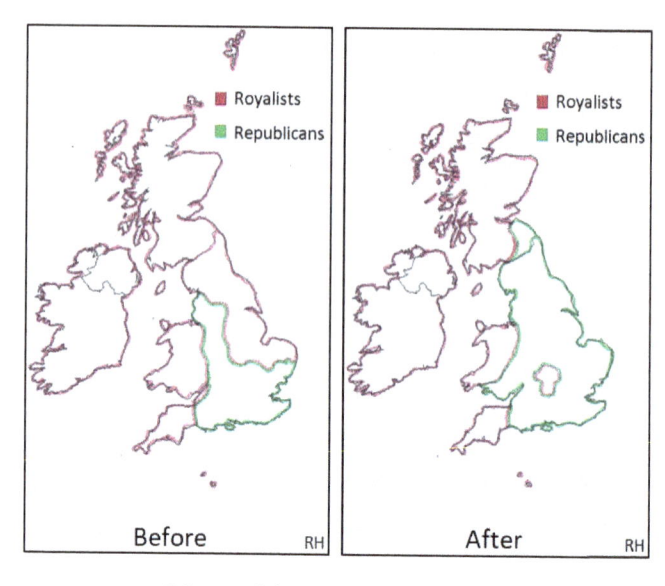

Maps of the English Civil war

In England, Cromwell was elected Lord Protector, essentially a Dictator. He ruled England through his Major Generals and a harsh interpretation of Puritanism. Hesitated a war with the Dutch due to trade rights and was severely unpopular when he died.

His son Richard Cromwell eventually renounced the Lord Protectorate and the Parliament voted to restore the Monarchy with Charles II as ruler. Charles agreed to the limitation of his power and agreed to share his rule with Parliament.

Charles also renewed relations with the Dutch and made a secret deal with Louis XIV to make his successor a catholic.

In 1666, London burned down during a fire that destroyed many ancient and historical land marks. The fire allowed for the redesigning of London in a more efficient way.

William III and Mary II coronation and oath to abide by the English Laws and rule with Parliament

Charles died with no legitimate heir, so his Brother, James became king. James angered the English people by being baptized as a Catholic and allying with France and Louis XIV. A nemesis of England.

His final hour came as he bore a son who was baptized as a Catholic, creating a Catholic dynasty.

This was the final straw for England, and so the Parliament invited the daughter of James, Mary and her husband the Price of Orange, William to invade England and restore Protestantism in England.

James fled to Ireland where he still had support. A war would ensue in Ireland and eventually James lost and fled with his son to France where he later died.

James' son would remain a pretender to the throne and created the idea of Jacobitism, the idea that he was the true king of England.

The overthrow of James was so revolutionary and fantastic in the eyes of England and thus it was dubbed, "The Glorious Revolution".

William and Mary agreed to adopt a constitutional monarchy and to create a Bill of Rights, in which every English citizen was protected by his natural rights as an Englishman.

William and Mary ruled jointly and peacefully until 1703 when the throne was passed on to Anne, the sister of Mary II.

Anne, due to her obesity and age, was hindered at her most important duty, producing an heir. However, Anne did some important things. She led England into the Spanish war of Succession, against France and united England and Scotland to form the Kingdom of Great Britain.

Anne knew she was the last of her kind and when she died, the Stuart Dynasty came to an end and her relative's child, George I of Hanover came to Britain and began the most powerful and corrupt era in British History, The Hanoverians.

House of Hanover

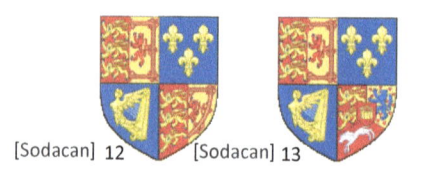

[Sodacan] 12   [Sodacan] 13   14   [Sodacan]

The death of Queen Anne led to the end of the Stuart Dynasty of Britain. The designated successor to Anne was Sophia of Hanover. Anne felt threatened and did not allow Sophia to come to England.

Queen Anne, the last Stuart and her rival Sophia of Hanover

Sophia unfortunately died before Queen Anne, so, her son, George came ascended to the throne. He spoke no English and in the Openings of parliament, George sat down in silence and a servant would read his text in English.

George also ended the War of Spanish Succession and thus he gave his country peace.

George's advantage was being a man and a soldier. George was seen like a warrior king and was greatly praised and idealized by writers like Daniel Defoe.

However, George also had issues to deal with. He was very quiet and somber. He had little character and was like a tree.

George was also too fond of Hanover. He would spend long periods of time away in Germany tending to the electorate of Hanover while Britain was left leaderless.

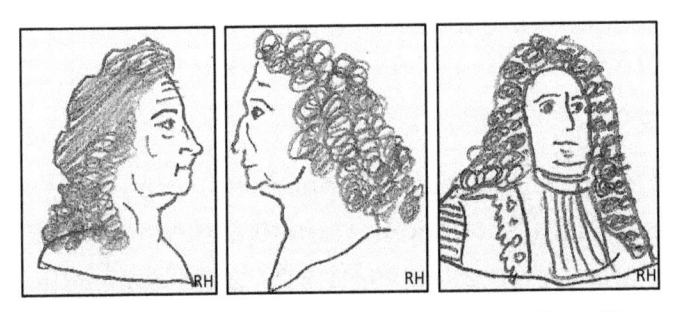

George I, his son, George II and Prime Minister Sir Robert Walpole

George ruled over a large Whig Ministry and got tangled in their affairs. George put his son, George Augustus, in charge of managing the biggest corporation in Britain at that time, the South Seas Company.

The company aimed to deal with Britain's debts but it failed spectacularly and brought Britain in to more debt, which it is still paying to this day.

The South Sea Bubble was a disaster for Britain and was a stain upon George I's reign.

This disaster also brought in a key figure in that era who helped deal with the immense amount of debt Britain acquired, he was Sir Robert Walpole, the First Prime Minister of Great Britain.

In 1715, seizing his opportunity, James II's son, James landed in Ireland and proclaimed himself, King James III. His coup against the new King George I eventually failed and James fled back to France, in exile, where he became known as the Old Pretender.

George also formed a tradition for the House of Hanover, Father-son Issues. George and his son the Prince of Wales hated each other and had little chemistry between them. In fact, The Prince of Wales detested his Father and often held a separate court from his Father.

George I forbade his son to take part in Court life and so George, The Prince of Wales was living in Richmond when he was given news of his father's passing.

Walpole personally came to see the Prince of Wales and gave George his father's will. George took it and put it in his pocket, where it was never seen again.

George II continued tradition by having a bad relationship with his son, Prince Fredrick.

The Prince of Wales, Fredrick

Fredrick often had his own court and noble would go to his court to peacefully oppose the King. This idea established a tradition that continues to this day in Parliament called His Majesty's most loyal opposition.

In 1739, George II took Britain to war against Spain in the War of Jenkin's Ear, an inconclusive war that just resulted in death and destruction.

George was at war with France. In the village of Dettingham, where he personally led the troops and inspired them with his words. This battle became the last instant in which an English or British king led his troops personally on the battlefield.

George also encountered an ancient foe. James II's grandson, Bonny Prince Charlie, the Stuart Jacobite pretender independently invaded Britain, landing in Scotland and naming himself, King Charles III. Charles summoned the Scottish clans and rallied them. Charles led his Jacobite Army south, where he hoped that George's unpopularity would lead England to proclaim him the new king.

The British army's early defeat near Edinburgh, rather than deprive the British from their loyalty to George, actually rallied them and soon a new large army marched north and decisively defeated Charles at the Battle of Collodion in 1746. This defeat drove Charles back to France and Jacobitism finally ended in Britain.

Jacobites would fight some time in Ireland but were eventually defeated, and George's throne was now secured.

George, in his later life, led Britain into the Seven Years war, a brutal conflict between all the major powers in Europe. Britain eventually won the war, seizing India, Canada and Ohio from France.

George died in 1760, leaving his throne to Fredrick's son George, who became the famous George III.

George was born in Britain but grew up in Hanover, where he learned how a European monarch should be like, powerful, caring and dutiful.

George's despotism led to anger in the streets of London and soon a peasant army marched off to Wimbledon to find the King, but they were eventually defeated.

King George III of Great Britain, Ireland and Hanover

George also presided over the rebellious North American colonies, who declared independence after a series of harsh taxes that were enforced to pay off Britain's debt from the seven years' war.

The war in America started off spiffy and Britain was poised to win the war. But disaster at Saratoga and at the siege of Yorktown and the fact that France and Spain joined the war on the American side brought the British army to the negotiating table. The Treaty of Paris ended the war and secured independence for the American Colonies, yet Canada stated loyal and faithful to Britain.

George blamed defeat in America to his own failure and suffered the first out of many instants of madness. The king was unable to function and was brutally treated by his doctors. But soon a much kinder method of treatment was found and George recovered just in time to face off Napoleon and the French Empire.

Britain would fight against France for eleven years until the Duke of Wellington, Arthur Wellesley defeated Napoleon and the Grand Army in a Battle just outside the village of Waterloo

Arthur Wellesley, The Duke of Wellington and his adversary, Napoleon Bonaparte

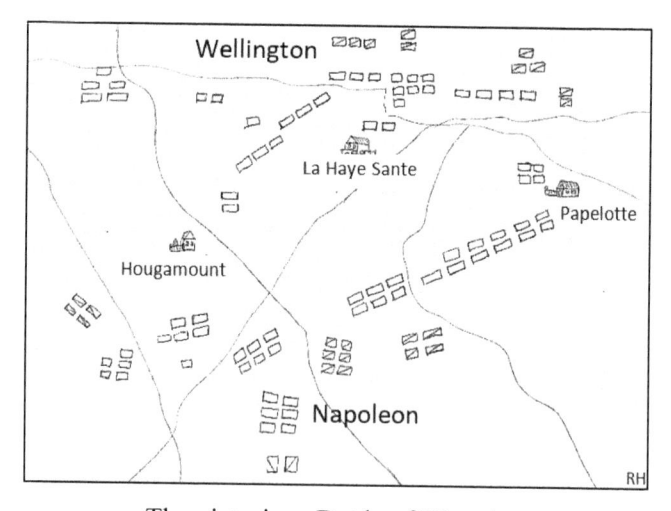

The victorious Battle of Waterloo

The defeat of "Bonny the Ogre", brought on a wave of patriotism and a new-found love for King George. George was incredibly popular as he was a kind-hearted king who loved his people.

In 1810 George suffered another episode of Madness and his mind collapsed. His son George "Prynne" Became prince Regent and was put in charge for the rest of George III's reign. George III died in 1820 an old and blind man after 60 years of rule, making him the longest reigning monarch up to that point.

Prynne was now in charge! George IV as he became known was incredibly hated and unpopular. In his time, as regent his carriage was mobbed and riots in London became overwhelming. A crackdown on rioters and the banning of unapproved meetings and assemblies were implemented.

George IV was also plagued by his unsuccessful marriage to his cousin Caroline of Brunswick. Their relationship was strained and unsuccessful and she was eventually divorced by the king, she was even locked out of the coronation. Their child, princess charlotte was a fresh start and she was destined for greatness as Queen but tragedy struck as she died suddenly.

In 1830, George's brother, William succeeded to the throne as William IV.

George IV, his wife Caroline and William IV

William was a navy man and had strict rules of etiquette. William was known for having a large amount of mistresses and a wave of illegitimate children but was eventually forced to make a legal marriage and it when smoothly.

He was very popular as he was very humble and even gave people a lift in his royal carriage, yet he was still conservative like any other Hanoverian King.

William opposed the move to increase suffrage and detested the Reform act of 1832 as he believed in the old ways of doing things. But he eventually had to restrain his ideas and Britain was started on to the road to Democracy.

After major reforms, the banning of rotten boroughs and reform of Parliament, the Monarchy could no longer manipulate Parliament and William was forced back into his constitutional box.

When William died in 1837, his throne went to his brother Edward, but he was dead. And so the throne went into the possession of an 18 year old girl, Victoria.

The Victorian Age

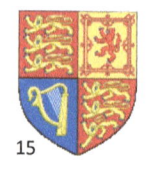

The death of William IV was a seminal moment. It signaled an end to the corrupt and misbehaving Hanoverians and marked the beginning of the age of modernization. Britain had begun a new wave of liberal reform such as in the Reform act of 1832 and other reforms on suffrage that were passed by the Whig dominated parliament that came into place after the Napoleonic Wars.

The throne went to Edward the Duke of Kent, the brother of King William IV, but he was dead at the time, so his crown went to his young daughter, Victoria.

Victoria was raised in Kensington Palace in complete isolation from the moment she was born. Her mother, Victoria of Saxe-Coberg saarfeld, was extremely fearful of the sinful nature of her evil uncles, George IV and William IV, and had the upmost intension to raise her daughter to be more civilized and kind in nature. And so, young Victoria grew up alone and had only her domineering mother and her lover as her companions. Victoria was only accompanied by the kindness of her dolls even as she grew up into a young woman.

Young Victoria

In 1837, at the age of 18, Victoria was told that William IV had died and that she was now Queen of the United Kingdom.

Victoria was hit hard by the news but was happy that she could finally move out of Kensington Palace and away from her mother.

Victoria rose to power during the Prime Ministry of the Lord Melbourne, the powerful Whig politician, who became a close companion of Victoria and one of her greatest advisors early in her reign.

Victoria was crowned on the 28 of June, 1838. The same year she met a dashing young prince, Albert, her first cousin and the son of the Duke of Sax-Coberg Gotha. Albert was straight, charming, responsible and handsome. Victoria is even quoted saying "he is excessively handsome, such beautiful eyes, my heart is quite going". They married in 1840. She was not very popular at the time, she even blocked a government change because it could upset her domestic affairs. The Prime Minister, Lord Melbourne had given his daughters of his supporters to be Victoria's maids of the bedchamber, but he was beaten in the Election by the Tory, Robert Peel, but Peel was forced to resign, and Melbourne returned to his post for a short while but eventually let his office.

Albert also took part in Victoria's Government. He dealt with revising and reforming affairs of the royal house and he further improved how palace life ran. The old gothic ways of doing things were now history. He also cut Victoria's costs dramatically and helped save money for public projects.

Albert directed the creation of the Crystal Palace, a huge greenhouse-like structure that would host the great exhibition of the work's arts and industry. This was a daunting task which he pulled off without breaking a sweat.

Prince Albert of Sax-Coburg Gotha

Albert's increasing involvement in government put an end to his popularity. Victoria wished he was given a title that was fit enough for his great works, according to her. He was given the title of Prince Consort, but he very much acted like a king.

Prince Albert master creation, the Crystal Palace

Albert very much worked himself to death. His last act as the 'king of Britain' was to intercept an angry dispatch to the American Government, by the Prime Minister. If it had been sent, Britain would have entered the American Civil War, on the side of the South.

Victoria entered a period of mourning that lasted the rest of her life. She hid away in Balmoral, a getaway she and Albert built for themselves.

Victoria and Albert's getaway, Balmoral

She did not open Parliament or participate in any of her regal duties and only allowed an audience to John Brown, an aide. She and Brown spent so much time together that she was referred to by the public as "Ms. Brown".

She still received an allowance from the government and yet she still did not play an active role in the running of the nation, which she should have been.

During this time, Britain was shaken by two great conflicts. The first was the Crimean war, which saw the involvement of France, under Napoleon III, Britain and the Ottoman Empire against the Russian Empire and their Tsar, Nicholas I. the was dragged out for three years and saw the death of many Britons, especially during the disastrous siege of Sevastopol, an important port for Russia in Crimea. The war ended with no territorial changes but it did nationalize the Black Sea.

The Second conflict at the time was the Sepoy Mutiny, in which Indian mercenaries for the British Army rebelled and temporarily took control of Delhi and crowned the Mughal Emperor, Bahadur Shah the Emperor of India. This revolt was put down with severity and Britain took direct control of India.

These conflicts were not of importance to the little Queen, she was still in hiding and in overarching sadness. Victoria need to get back into court life and rise again out of the tragedy that was Albert's death.

This time was very tenuous and Victoria almost lost her throne, if it wasn't for her children. No one in government wanted to scrap Victoria because her children were the most important diplomatic tool of the British nation. Victoria's children would marry into other royal families of Europe and thus forge a sturdy bond with the nation that had participated in the Marriage.

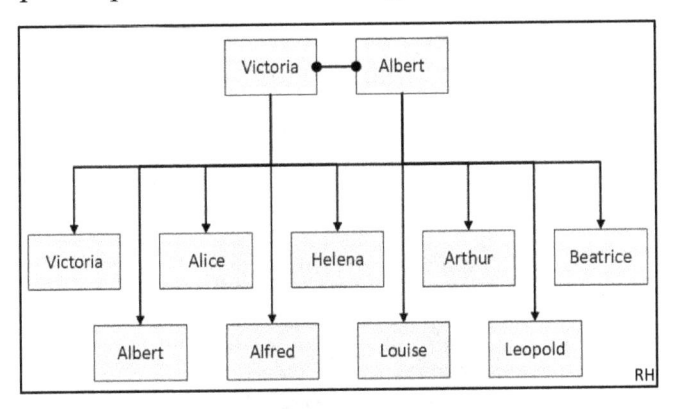

Victoria and Albert's Children

Victoria was finally given new life when the Tories took control of Parliament. Enter, Benjamin Disraeli, a cunning and charming man who had a way of making Victoria love being Queen once again. He made her Empress of India, a title she was very flattered to have. He made her appear as the great matriarch sovereign, the mother of the nation. Disraeli made her the logo of Britain and its Empire, putting her on stamps, coins and other little items.

Victoria had risen to prominence once again and she was well beloved. The later part of her reign saw a rise in the economic might of Britain and saw its empire expand as South Africa was conquered from the Zulus and Boers, Dutch people of South Africa.

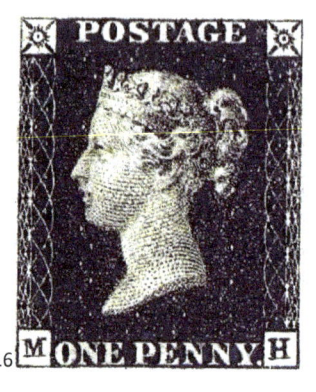

The iconic Victoria stamp, the rarest in the world, a symbol of her new status as Britain's icon

Victoria also forged relations with other powers of Europe. The new united Germany had married into the Royal Family as Victoria's daughter married the Kaiser, Fredrick III, and thus his son, the next Kaiser, Wilhelm II was Victoria's grandson. Wilhelm would admire his Grandmother for the rest of his life and sought to model his nation after her realm.

Victoria was also the longest reigning monarch up to that time, 63 years on the throne. She reigned for so long that people hardly remembered what came before her.

Victoria led her nation into the new century, as the British Empire was at the peak of its power, fame and glory.

Yet Victoria was getting old, and just twenty one days into the new century, Victoria fell ill and died after 63 years on the throne of Britain. Her reign was the most glorious and prosperous in British history and is often called splendid isolation, or the Pax Britannica, or British Peace.

The British Nation would have to strive into the Twentieth century without the security of the great mother hen.

House of Windsor

The death of Queen Victoria sent shockwaves across Europe. In a matter of hours, the Queen that ruled longer than any other left the Kingdom. Victoria's son, Albert was now crowned, Edward VII, the first king Britain had in over 63 years.

Victoria would cast a long shadow, and a legacy that would seem unmatchable. Edward was already 59 years old, was fat and unhealthy, smoking and drinking frequently.

The funeral of Queen Victoria and the Coronation of Edward VII would involve the creation of tradition, as those ceremonies have not been exercised in over half a century.

Edward was a lively person. He was prone to gambling, smoking, drinking and entertaining. Yet as he came to the throne he yearned to create a whole new image for himself.

Edward was also extremely tolerant for his time. He enjoyed the company of others such as Jews, Catholics and other races that were misunderstood in the empire. Edward is quoted saying "because a man has a black face or a different religion then our own, there is no reason he should be treated as a brute."

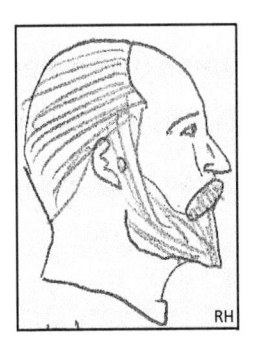

Britain's new and Jolly King, Edward VII

He worked on various reforms regarding Labour and housing, and even invited working class people to stay at Sandringham Palace, although he was not allowed to eat in the dining hall, due to a lack of proper clothing.

Edward pictured himself as a nursery rhyme monarch, a kind, happy and helpful monarch, that works only for the joy of his people.

Edward also travelled to France to initiate an alliance that became the Entante Cordial, an alliance between France, Britain and Russia, this would become extremely important in 1914.

This alliance isolated Germany, as Edward detested his nephew, the Kaiser of Germany.

Edward convinced the press to back a treaty that stated that if France was attacked, Britain would go to war.

Edward also opposed voting rights for women or any reform on suffrage.

During his reign, income taxes were created to fund the creation of old age pensions for retired labourers, a bill proposed by future PM, David Lloyd George.

The Tories in government firmly detested the so-called "Peoples Bill." To pass such an act, new peers in government would have to be created and Edward was firmly opposing this.

In May 1910, as turmoil filled the whole of parliament, Edward died.

That same year, Edward's 44-year-old son, George inherited the throne from his father. George was Edward's second son and grew up a navy man and was deeply attached to his naval position, but when his older brother Clarence died, he became heir.

George also married Clarence's fiancé, Mary of Teck, and so he inherited a fortune of about 140 million pounds in today's currency, and a crisis.

The battle to pass the people's budget was came out with the result that the King would pay no income tax, and in return the King would pay for any trips abroad himself.

George also inherited his father's Entante treaty, and in July 1914 it all came to a head.

The archduke of Austria was murdered by a Serbian Nationalist. Austria sent an ultimatum that was purposely made to fail. And so, Austria declared war on Serbia. Because of an old alliance, Russia declared war on Austria and because of the Austro-German alliance, Germany declared war on Russia. Because of the Entante Cordial, France declared war on Germany, and because Germany violated Belgium's neutrality by invading them as a part of the Schlieffen plan, Britain declared war on Germany, and thus the Great War began.

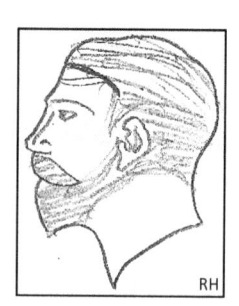

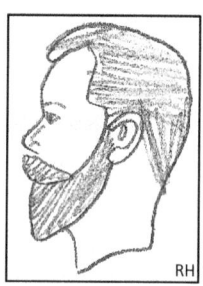

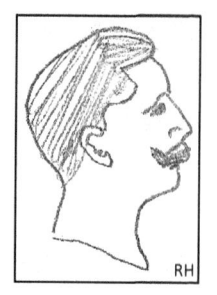

George V and his two cousins, Tsar Nicholas II and the German Kaiser Wilhelm II

But George had an unnerving issue. His family was of German origin and his own last name was Sax- Coberg Gotha, a German duchy. George was also Field Marshall of the Prussian Army and Admiral General of the German Navy.

An so, George systematically purged his German titles, honours and his own last name, from Sax Coberg Gotha, to Windsor, which was a stereotypically English sounding name.

George was now the peoples King, a truly English Monarch and not a German sympathizer.

The Western Front in Belgium and France saw much brutality as new mechanized war machines such as the Tank and Airplane, clashed against the old tactic of the European Nations.

British and ANZAC forces made a disastrous invasion of Gallipoli in Turkey and Britain also established a large military force that invaded throughout Iraq and Palestine.

At this time, British lord, Arthur Balfour, published the Balfour declaration, stating that a Jewish State in Palestine was in the agenda of the British Government.

Britain also intercepted the Zimmerman telegram, a message from Germany to Mexico, urging them to invade the southern United States in exchange for land. Britain, after much consideration, forwarded the telegram to the American Government and soon after, the United States joined the Allied forces and declared war on Germany.

The Great War ended on November 11th, 1918 with the treaty of Versailles, which negotiated harsh terms with Germany which it would forever resent.

George and his Empire also increased in size as former German colonies in Cameroon, Tanzania, Namibia and Papua New Guinea were annexed.

After the war, a mutiny of sailors sprang up but was put down by the King himself and Admiral Kelly. To this day the full role and powered the King could hold and had held is a secret.

George had two sons, Edward the Prince of Wales, who was rash and indecisive, and Albert, his favorite.

In 1923, Albert married the young and pretty Elizabeth Bowes Lyon and three years later, in 1926 they had produced a young Girl, her name was Elizabeth. Although it was not the plan, this young girl and her father Albert would both be monarchs due to a twist of fate.

George also used the new power of technology. In 1932, George made history by broad casting the first Christmas message from the King via radio, an evolutionary method of communication, which George was quick to take advantage of.

In 1936, at the age of 70, George V died and left his Kingdom to his unruly son, Edward.

George was quoted saying that after Edward came to the throne "he would ruin himself in a month."

King Edward VIII

Quickly young Edward VIII got himself into trouble. He fell in love with Wallis Simpson, an American commoner and a double divorce. Due to his role as King of Britain and head of the Church of England, Edward was forbidden from marrying Wallis. The only way he could marry his true love, was by abdicating and leaving Britain forever, which he did, leaving the Crown to his younger brother Albert.

Albert, know George VI, was a shy and nervous man, who did not want to be King, he was prone to stutter and was a bad public speaker. George was aided through these challenges by a mentor and smoking.

One of the most important King in British History, King George VI

George also presided over Britain's darkest hour. In Europe, Hitler and his Nazi Party took power in Germany and were quickly able to overwhelm Austria, Czechoslovakia and eventually Poland with the new German Army and its highly experienced Generals.

Germany also invaded France and North Africa. In France, the Allies made a retreat to Britain at Dunkirk. In Africa, Britain faced the desert fox, Erwin Rommel, but Britain had a weapon of its own, General Montgomery. Montgomery led the defeat of Rommel and the German army in Tunisia and eventually was one of the commanders of the invasion of Italy.

Over Britain, the German air force and the RAF fought the Battle of Britain in 1940. Which saw to large bombings of London by German Heinkel Bombers. Germany would eventually lost the Battle of Britain, but would unleash the Blitz, a bombing campaign of London and other cities in Britain, even the Palace of the King was bombed, but the king held his head high and kept cool in order to comfort his devastated people through the hard times.

In 1944, Operation Overlord was enacted, a large invasion force of Normandy by the allied forces. This invasion was successful and in the long run ended German domination of Europe. Paris was liberated in 1944. On April 30th, Hitler committed suicide and on May 8th, 1945, Berlin was captured and Germany signed and armistice. In the Pacific, Britain, along with the United States fought a long war against Japan which ended in August of 1945 after two atomic bombs were dropped on Hiroshima and Nagasaki.

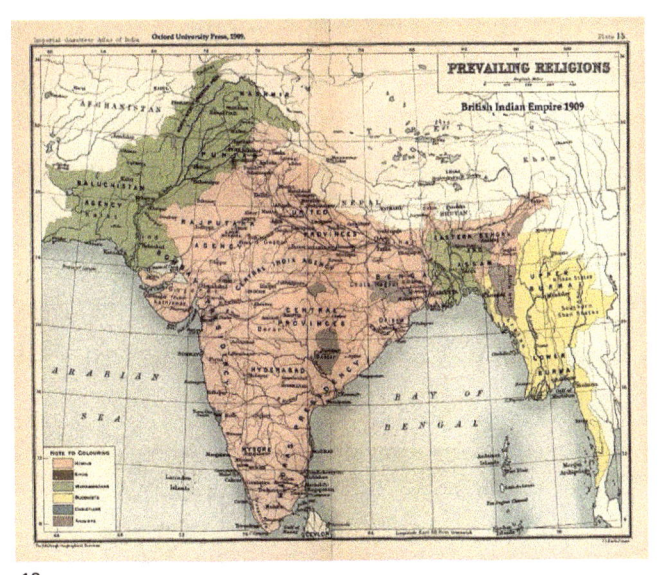

Partition of India

The Second World War came to an end, and thus Britain's Empire began to crumble. In India, the Viceroy, Lord Louis Mountbatten, had called a vote to ask if people wished to make India independent and it's passed. India and Pakistan became dominions and the Indian Empire collapsed and so was George's title of Emperor. India would later end its dominionship in favor of complete independence.

The pressures of the War and the subsequent breakup of Britain's Empire, along with his smoking habits, drained the Kings health and in 1952, George VI died passing his throne to a young 26 year old former mechanic during the Second World War, Elizabeth II. In 1953, Elizabeth was crowned the first Queen since Victoria and her reign in still ongoing.

Coronation portrait of Queen Elizabeth II

Britain loves her Queen and the whole world wishes her a happy 91st Birthday in March. God Save the Queen.

The Queen is currently the longest reigning monarch in English History, beating out Victoria in 2014.

The Queen was also a mechanic during WWII and an active service officer.

The summarizing of the Reign of Queen Elizabeth II is not currently possible due to her reign being ongoing and thus it has not been closed by history.

Appendices

House of Normandy

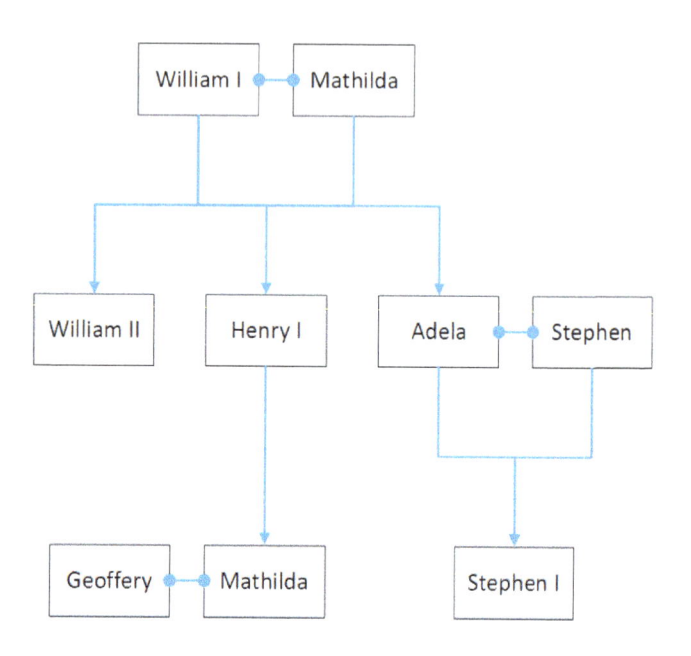

```
        William I —— Mathilda
              |
   ┌──────────┼──────────┐
William II  Henry I    Adela —— Stephen
              |                   |
       Geoffery —— Mathilda    Stephen I
```

House of Plantagenet

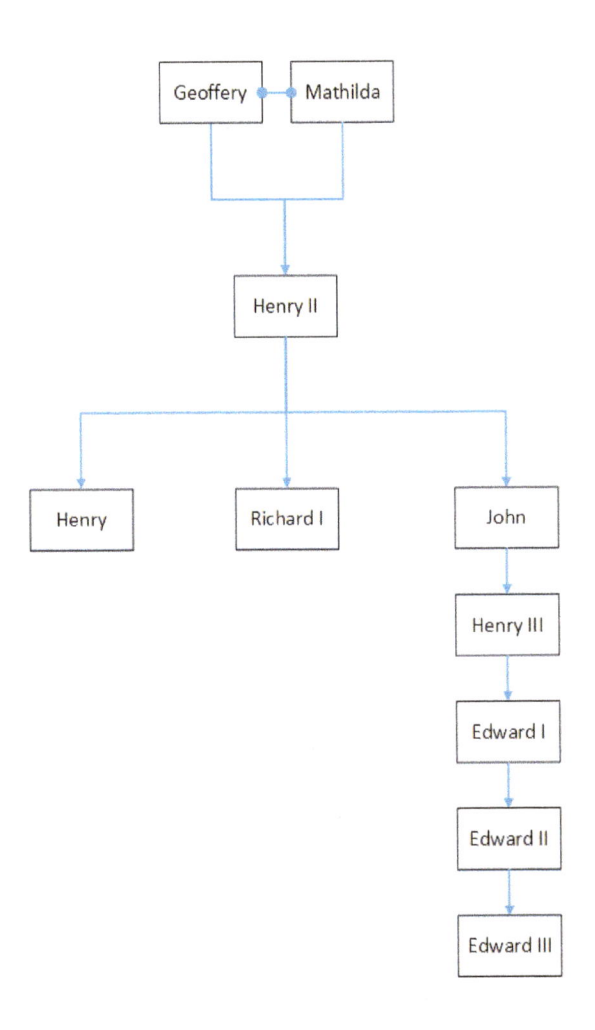

```
Geoffery —— Mathilda
         │
      Henry II
         │
   ┌─────┼─────┐
 Henry  Richard I  John
                   │
                Henry III
                   │
                Edward I
                   │
                Edward II
                   │
                Edward III
```

House of Tutor

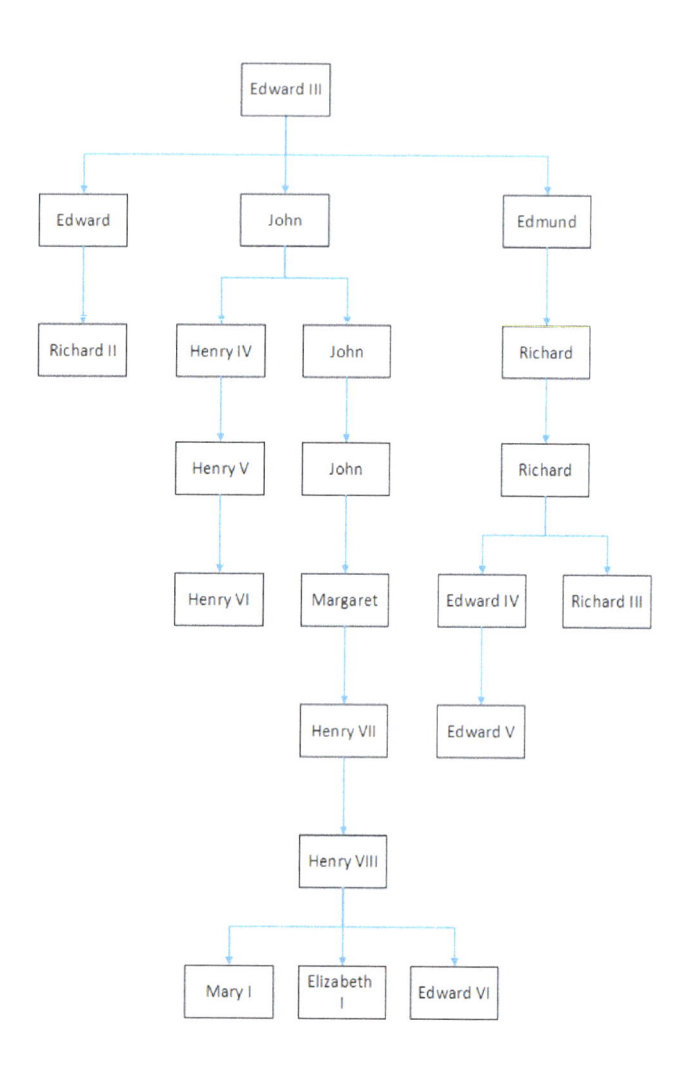

- Edward III
  - Edward
    - Richard II
  - John
    - Henry IV
      - Henry V
        - Henry VI
    - John
      - John
        - Margaret
          - Henry VII
            - Henry VIII
              - Mary I
              - Elizabeth I
              - Edward VI
  - Edmund
    - Richard
      - Richard
        - Edward IV
          - Edward V
        - Richard III

House of Stuart

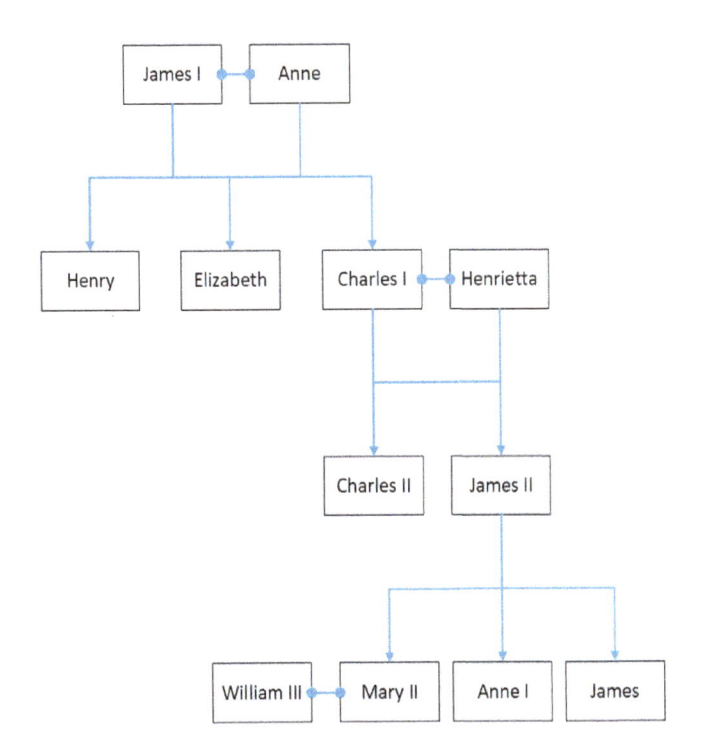

```
James I ── Anne
   │
   ├── Henry
   ├── Elizabeth
   └── Charles I ── Henrietta
            │
            ├── Charles II
            └── James II
                   │
                   ├── Mary II ── William III
                   ├── Anne I
                   └── James
```

House of Hanover

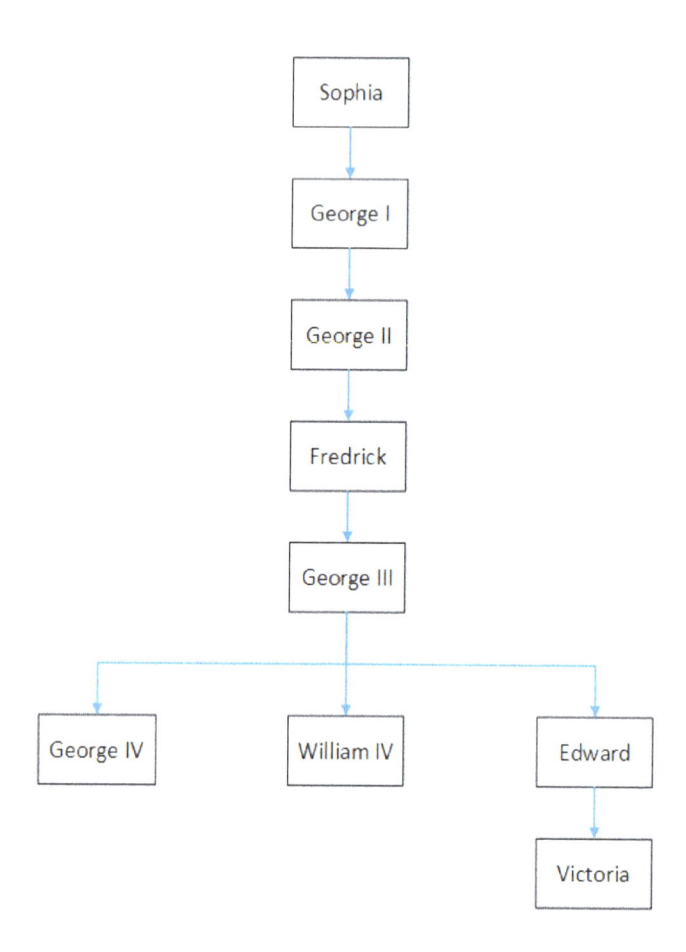

- Sophia
  - George I
    - George II
      - Fredrick
        - George III
          - George IV
          - William IV
          - Edward
            - Victoria

House of Windsor

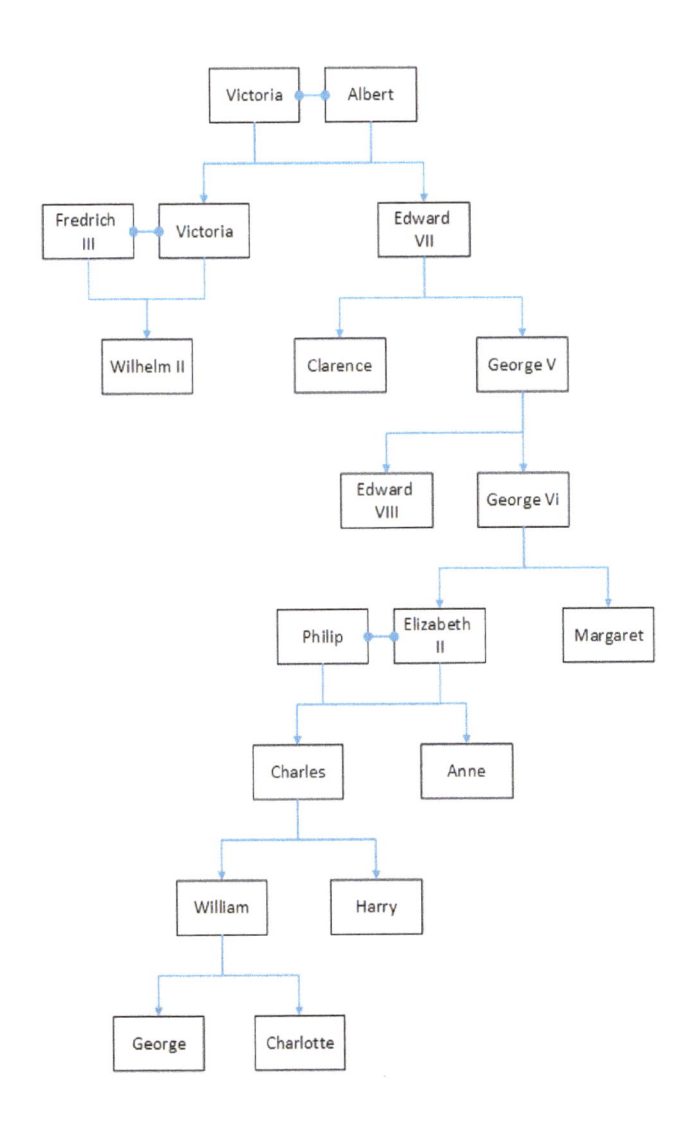

- Victoria — Albert
  - Victoria — Fredrich III
    - Wilhelm II
  - Edward VII
    - Clarence
    - George V
      - Edward VIII
      - George Vi
        - Elizabeth II — Philip
          - Charles
            - William
              - George
              - Charlotte
            - Harry
          - Anne
        - Margaret

References

Information used in the creation of this piece are from:

- Bodleian Library, University of Oxford
- University of Cambridge Library
- New Britain Public Library
- The History of England by Rapin de Thoyras
- The English and Their History by Robert Tombs
- Lucy Worsley Fit to Rule Documentary series
- Wikipedia, The free encyclopedia

The images and drawings that appear in this book were created by the author, except those that are numbered. The images that are numbered are either a public domain images or are the work of [another creator] and those images were given permission, by the creator, to be used under specific conditions that are outlined here:

01	A segment of the Bayeux Tapestry depicting Odo, Bishop of Bayeux, rallying Duke William's troops during the Battle of Hastings in 1066	Public Domain File: Odo bayeux tapestry.png Uploaded: 5 April 2006 [Myrabella]
02	Coat of arms of Sark, part of Guernsey	Public Domain view terms File: Escudo de Sark.svg Uploaded: 9 January 2008 [Xinese-v]
03	Royal Arms of England (1198 - 1340)	CC BY-SA 4.0 view terms File: Royal Arms of England (1198-1340).svg Created: 20 July 2010 [Sodacan]
04	The Angevin Empire map	CC BY-SA 3.0 File: Henry II, Plantagenet Empire.png Created: 31 December 2007 [Cartedaos]
05	A map of the Third Crusade	License: Creative Commons Attribution-Share Alike 4.0 [Kandi]
06	Magna Carta	Public Domain File: Magna Carta, British Library Cotton MS Augustus II 106.jpg [PiaCarott]
07	Royal Arms of England and France (1470-1471)	CC BY-SA 3.0 view terms File: Royal Arms of England (1470-1471).svg Created: 20 July 2010 [Sodacan]
08	Royal Arms of England and France used intermittently (1399-1603)	CC BY-SA 3.0 view terms File: Royal Arms of England (1399-1603).svg Created: 20 July 2010 [Sodacan]
09	Royal Arms of England (1603-1707)	CC BY-SA 3.0 view terms File: Royal Arms of England (1603-1707).svg Created: 20 July 2010 [Sodacan]
10	Royal Arms of England (1689-1694)	CC BY-SA 3.0 view terms File: Royal Arms of England (1689-1694).svg Created: 20 July 2010 [Sodacan]
11	Royal Arms of England (1694-1702)	CC BY-SA 3.0 view terms File: Royal Arms of England (1694-1702).svg Created: 20 July 2010 [Sodacan]

12	Royal Arms of Great Britain, France and Ireland (1707-1714)	CC BY-SA 3.0 view terms File: Royal Arms of Great Britain (1707-1714).svg Created: 20 July 2010 [Sodacan]
13	Royal Arms of Great Britain, France, Ireland, Hanover, and Brunswick (1714-1801)	CC BY-SA 3.0 view terms File: Royal Arms of Great Britain (1714-1801).svg Created: 20 July 2010 [Sodacan]
14	Royal Shield of Arms of the Kingdom of Hanover	CC BY-SA 3.0 view terms File: Royal Arms of the Kingdom of Hanover.svg Created: 9 October 2010 [Sodacan]
15 17	Arms of the United Kingdom of Great Britain and Northern Ireland	CC BY-SA 3.0 File: Arms of the United Kingdom.svg Created: 20 July 2010 [Sodacan]
16	The Penny Black, Great Britain, 1840	Public Domain File: Penny black.jpg Created: 1 May 1840
17	See 15	
18	Partition of India Map	Public Domain File: Brit IndianEmpireReligions3.jpg Created: 31 December 1908
19	Coronation portrait of Queen Elizabeth II	Public Domain view terms File: Elizabeth II & Philip after Coronation.JPG Created: 1 June 1953

Lightning Source UK Ltd.
Milton Keynes UK
UKHW022137130521
383686UK00006B/83

9 783743 935273